UNDER THE MICROSCOPE

EARTH'S TINIEST INHABITANTS

Soil Science for Kids
Children's Earth Sciences Books

BABY PROFESSOR
EDUCATION KIDS

Speedy Publishing LLC
40 E. Main St. #1156
Newark, DE 19711
www.speedypublishing.com

n this book, we're going to cover some basics about soil and all the different types of microorganisms that live in it. So, let's get right to it!

The soil under our feet is filled with organisms. Some of them you can see if you hold some soil in the palm of your hand and others are so tiny that you can't see them without a microscope. There are so many microorganisms in one teaspoon of soil that they outnumber the people on Earth!

Dirt.

A close-up of white mould on soil.

WHAT IS A MICROORGANISM?

A microorganism is an extremely small organism that can only be seen with a microscope. As long as there is some source of carbon for energy, the populations of these different microorganisms thrive in the soil. Some of them are hardier than others, which simply means they can exist under less than ideal conditions.

For example, bacteria, protozoa, and actinomycetes can tolerate a lot of disturbance of the soil, so if a farmer tills the soil, they can still live there and thrive. Fungi and nematodes thrive better in soils that haven't been tilled.

Inedible mushrooms growing in the green grass.

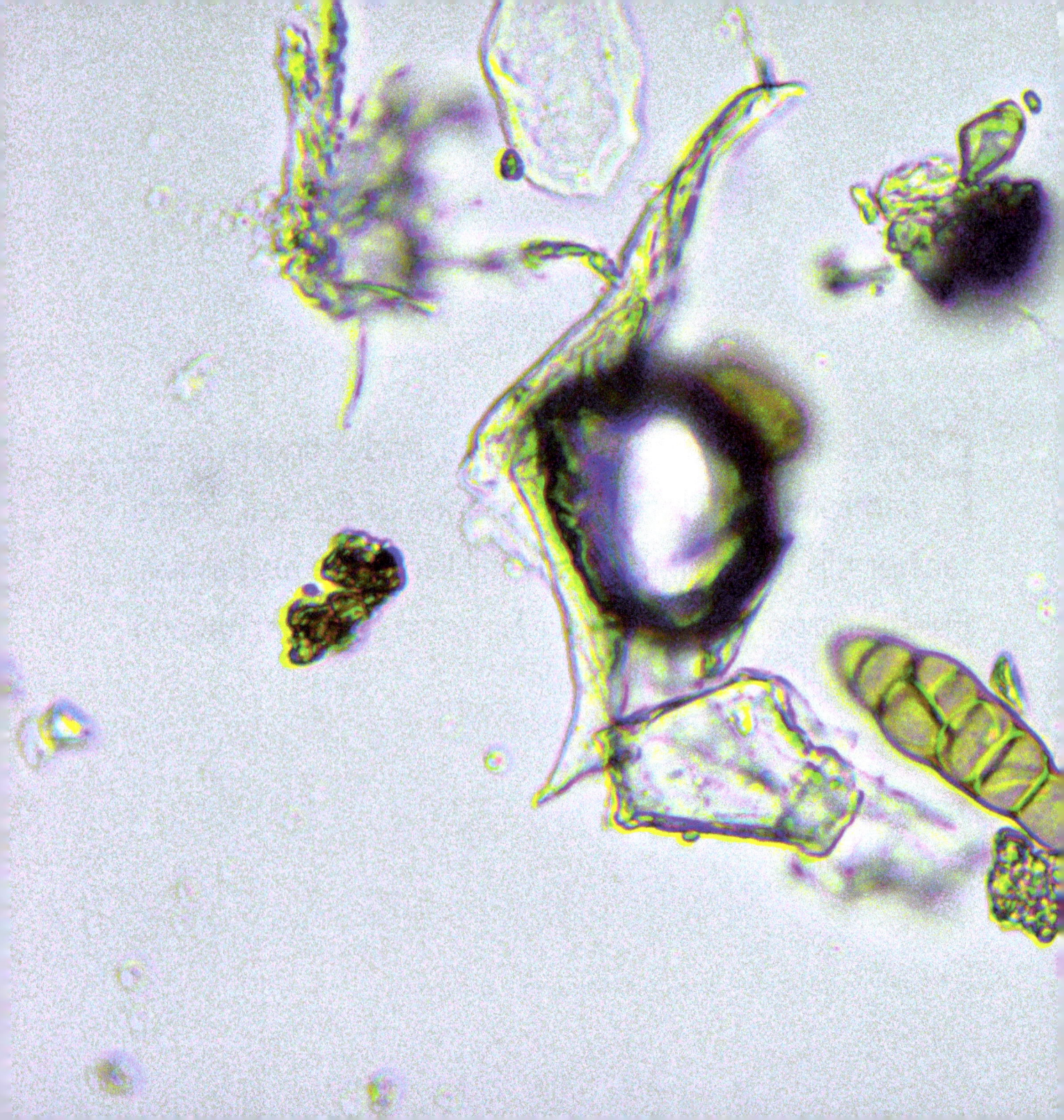

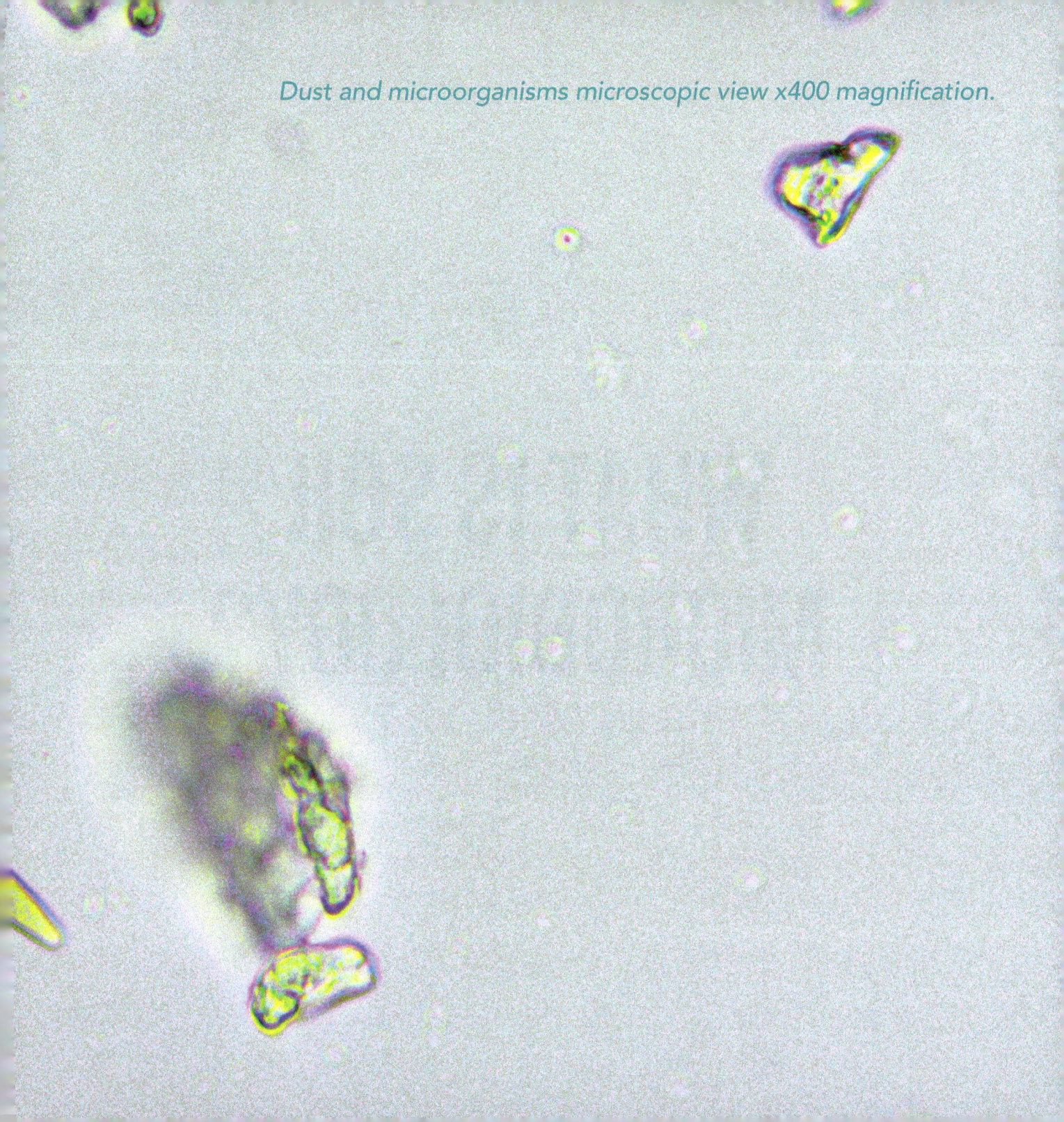
Dust and microorganisms microscopic view x400 magnification.

WHAT IS SOIL MICROBIOLOGY?

Soil microbiology is the science of microorganisms and how these organisms interact with the soil. Billions of years ago, primitive bacteria and microorganisms were alive in the oceans of Earth. Eventually, they adapted to live on land as well.

These bacteria were able to fix nitrogen, which simply means they could convert nitrogen into other types of molecules needed for living organisms. Over a long period of time, these microorganisms thrived and released oxygen. This process led to microorganisms that were even more advanced.

The microorganisms in our soil are very important because they affect the structure of the soil as well as its fertility. Fertile soil yields more food for animals and people and helps plants grow. Each group of microorganisms has a specific function in the soil.

Plants background with biochemistry structure.

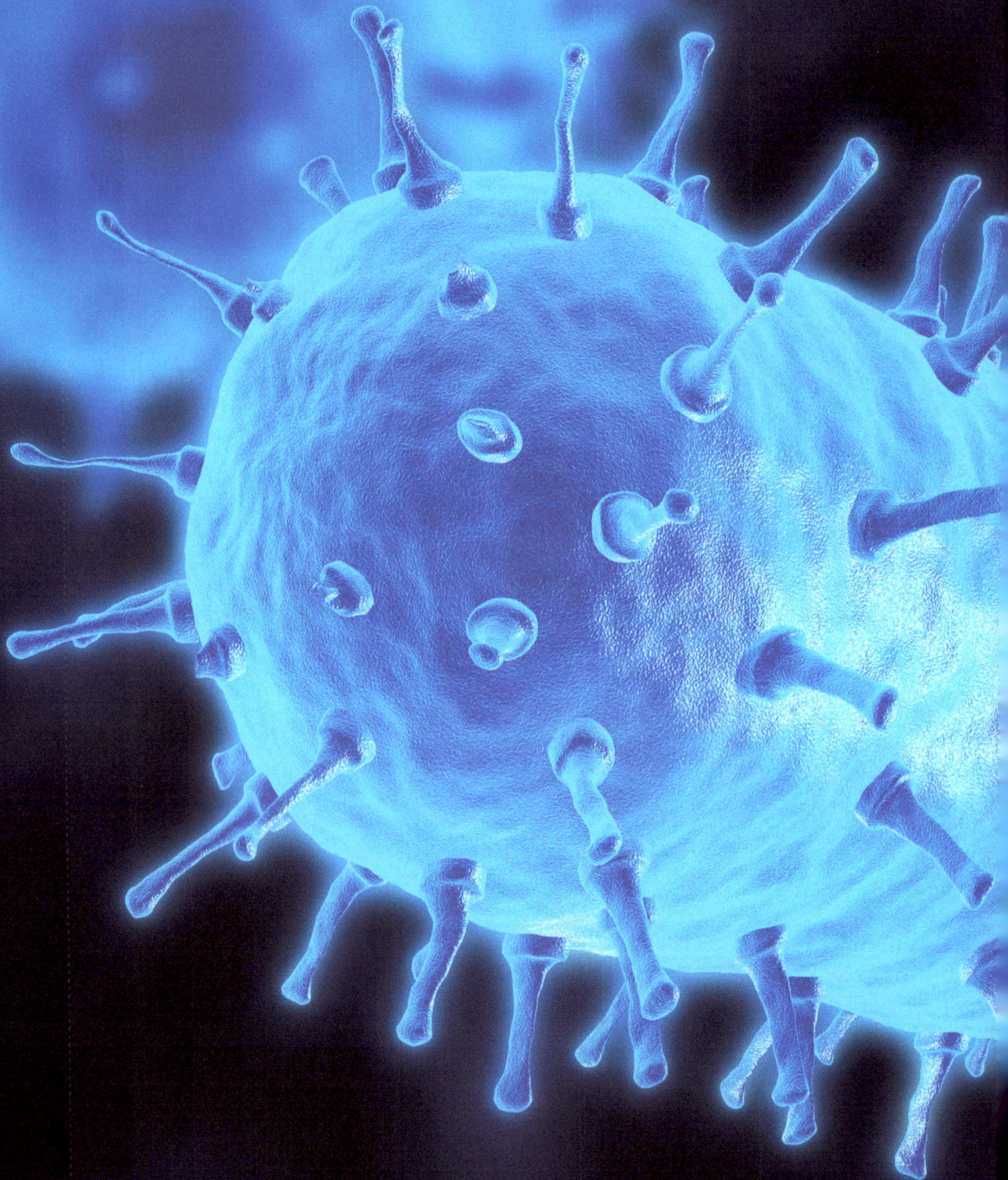

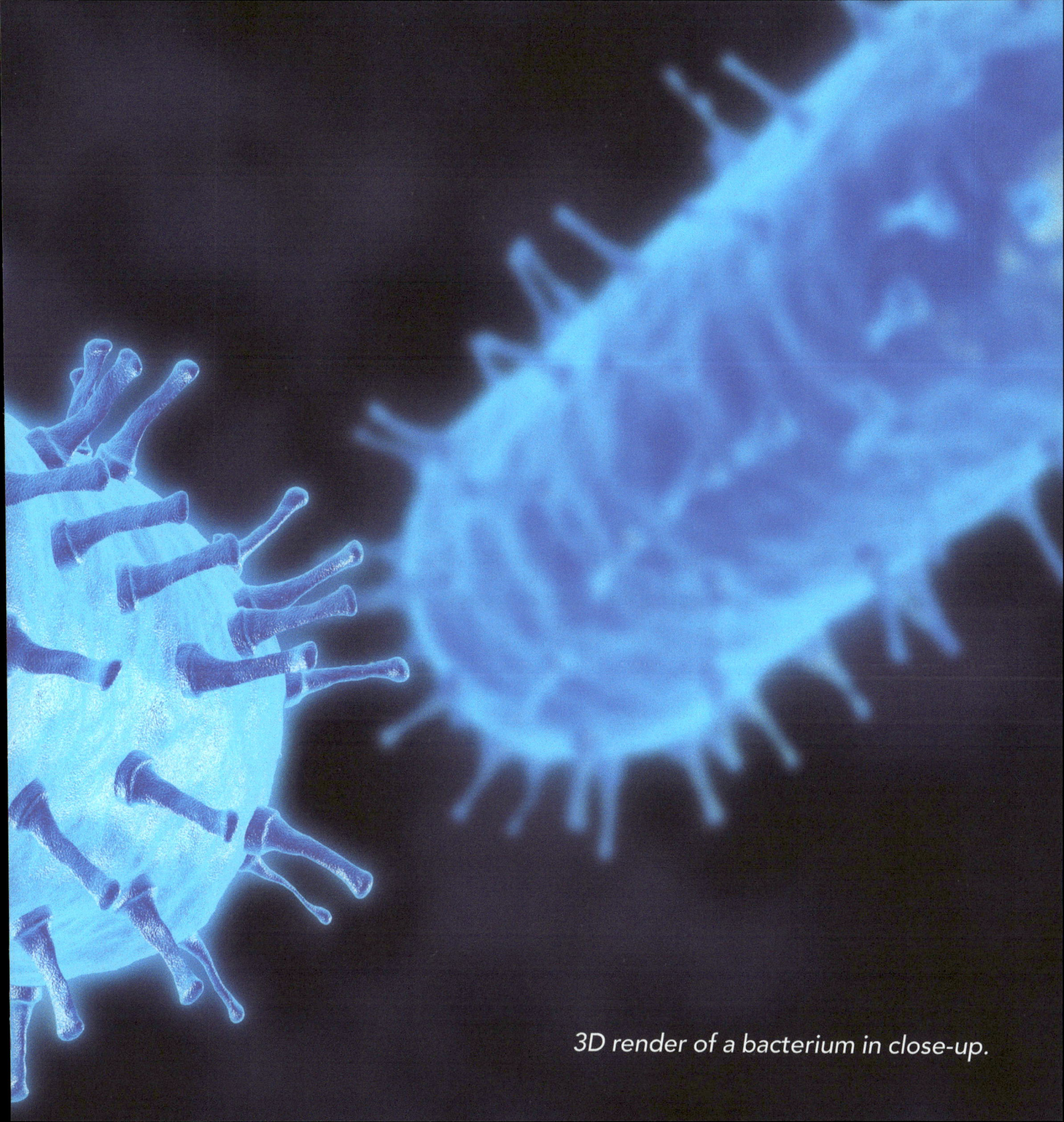

3D render of a bacterium in close-up.

BACTERIA

Bacteria and also **Archaea**, which are very similar to bacteria, are the tiniest organisms that live in soil other than viruses. They are prokaryotic. This means that they have the simplest type of cell structure. Their cells don't have a nucleus that tells the cell what to do. Their cell walls are similar to plant cells. If you saw them under a microscope you would notice that they are all different shapes. Some look like spheres. Others are rods and spirals. Some even have long *"Tails"* that are called **Flagella**. Even though bacteria and their *"Cousins"* archaea are the smallest organisms found in soil other than viruses, they are also the most abundant.

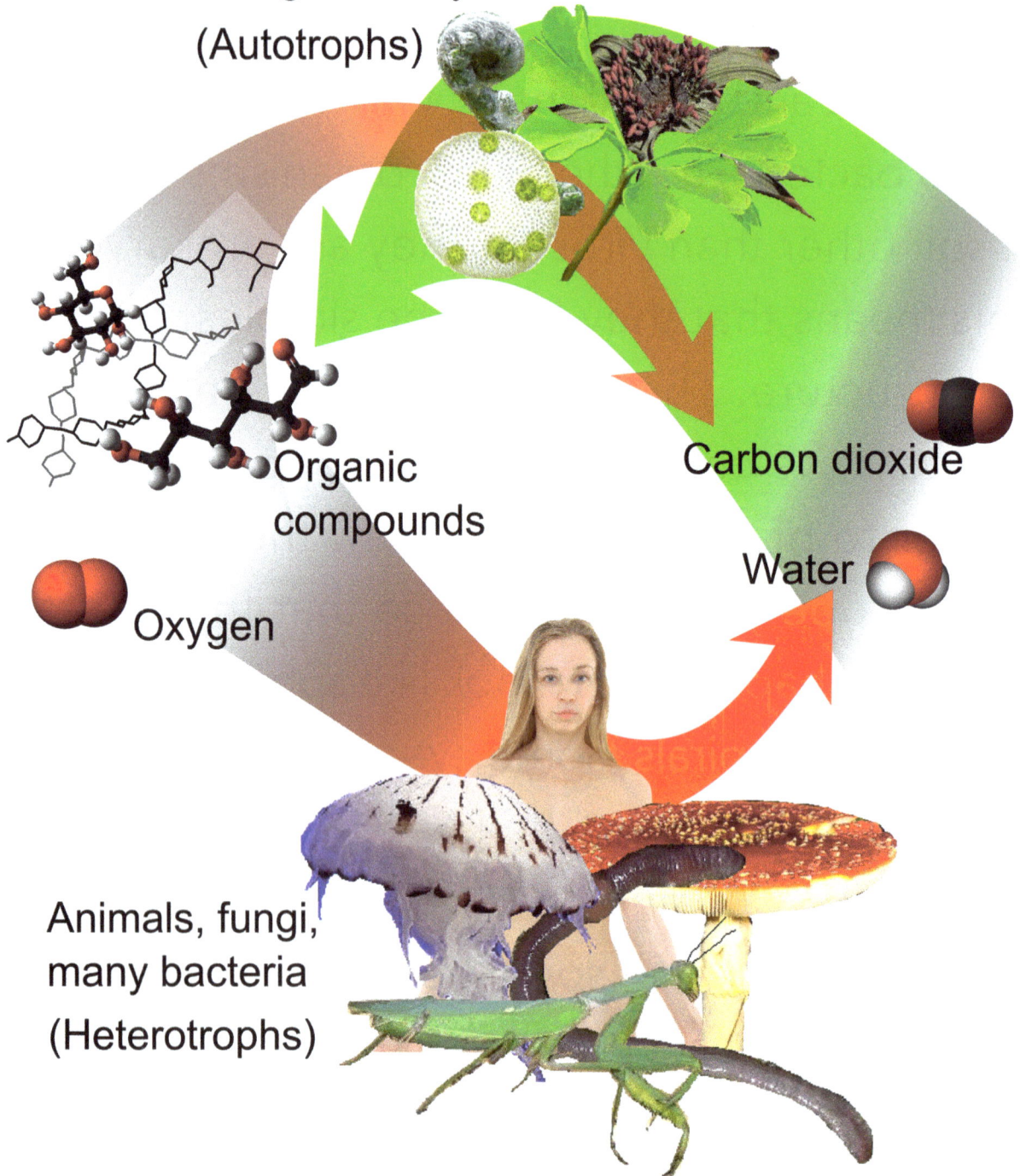

Plants, algae, many bacteria
(Autotrophs)

Organic
compounds

Carbon dioxide

Water

Oxygen

Animals, fungi,
many bacteria
(Heterotrophs)

Bacteria are vitally important to the process of life on Earth. Some bacteria are decomposers. They break down dead material from both animals and plants. This process creates fertile soil and gets rid of waste materials.

There are two major categories of bacteria: *Autotrophic* and *Heterotrophic.*

- **Autotrophic Bacteria** create their own food through a process called oxidation.

- **Heterotrophic Bacteria** get their food from plants or other microorganisms.

Cycle between autotrophs and heterotrophs.

The amount of autotrophic bacteria in the soil is much smaller than heterotrophic. However, autotrophic bacteria are highly important because they convert nitrogen from the air to compounds that plants and other organisms need to survive.

Prokaryote cell with structure and parts.

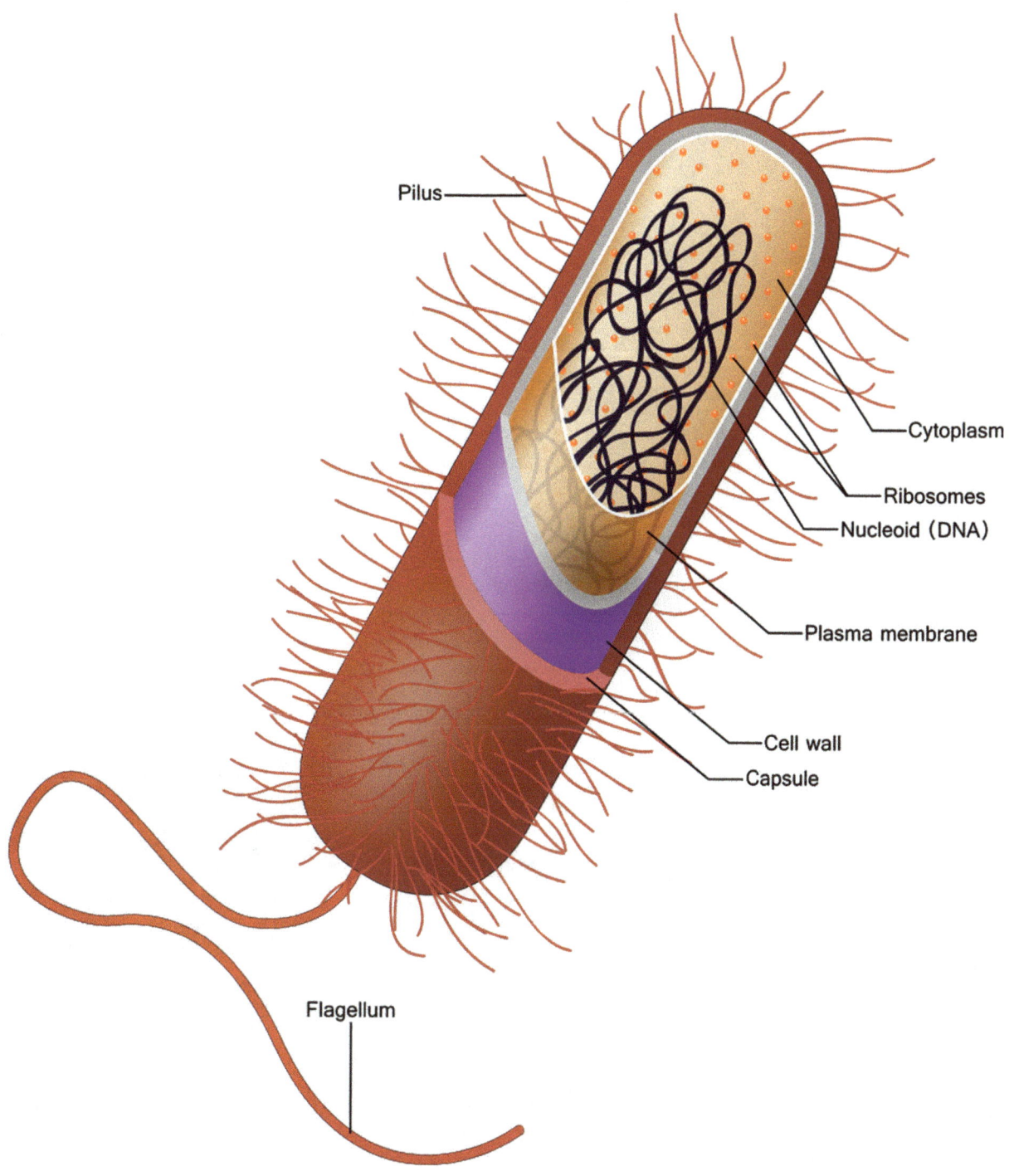

Pilus

Cytoplasm

Ribosomes

Nucleoid (DNA)

Plasma membrane

Cell wall

Capsule

Flagellum

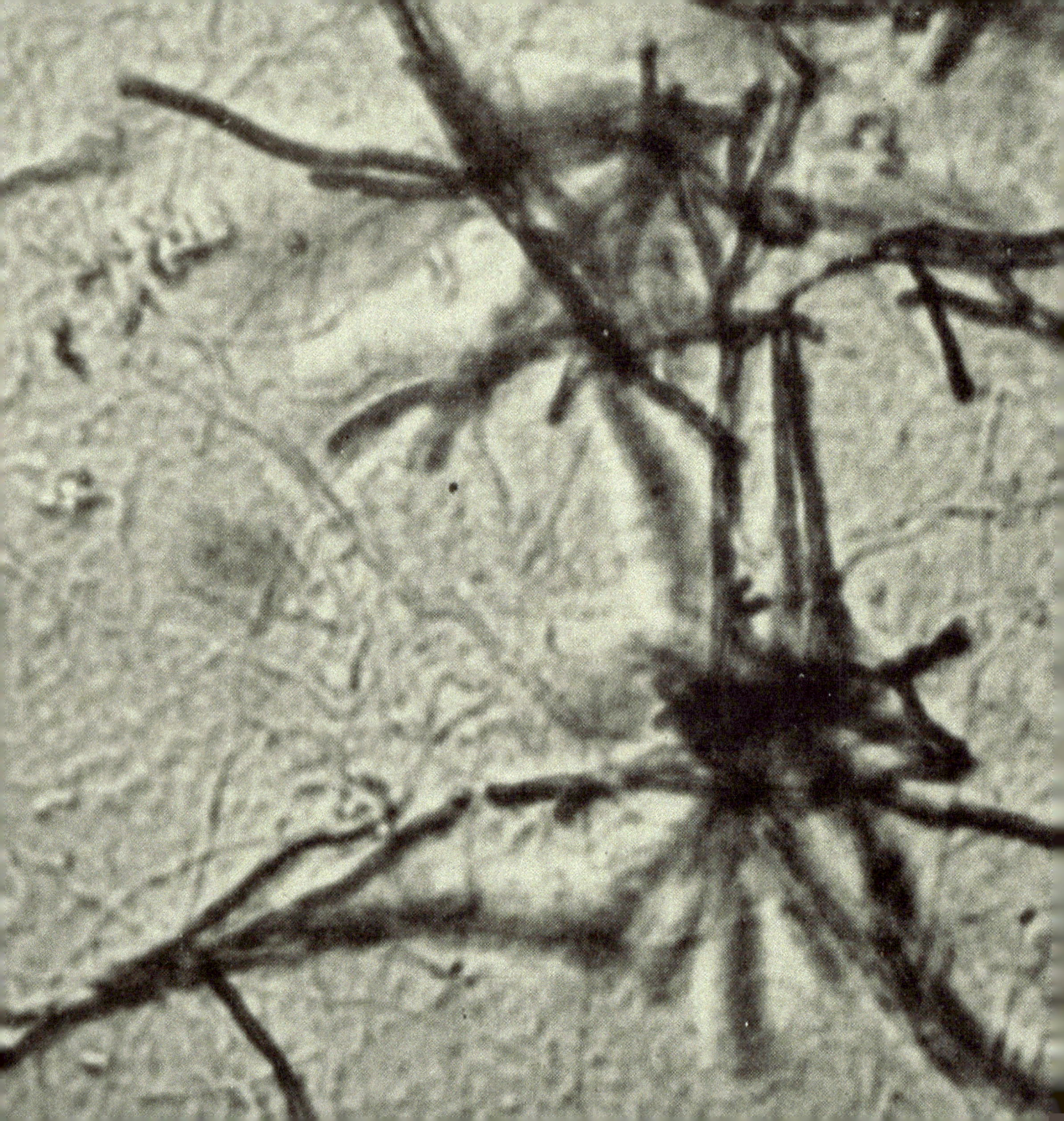

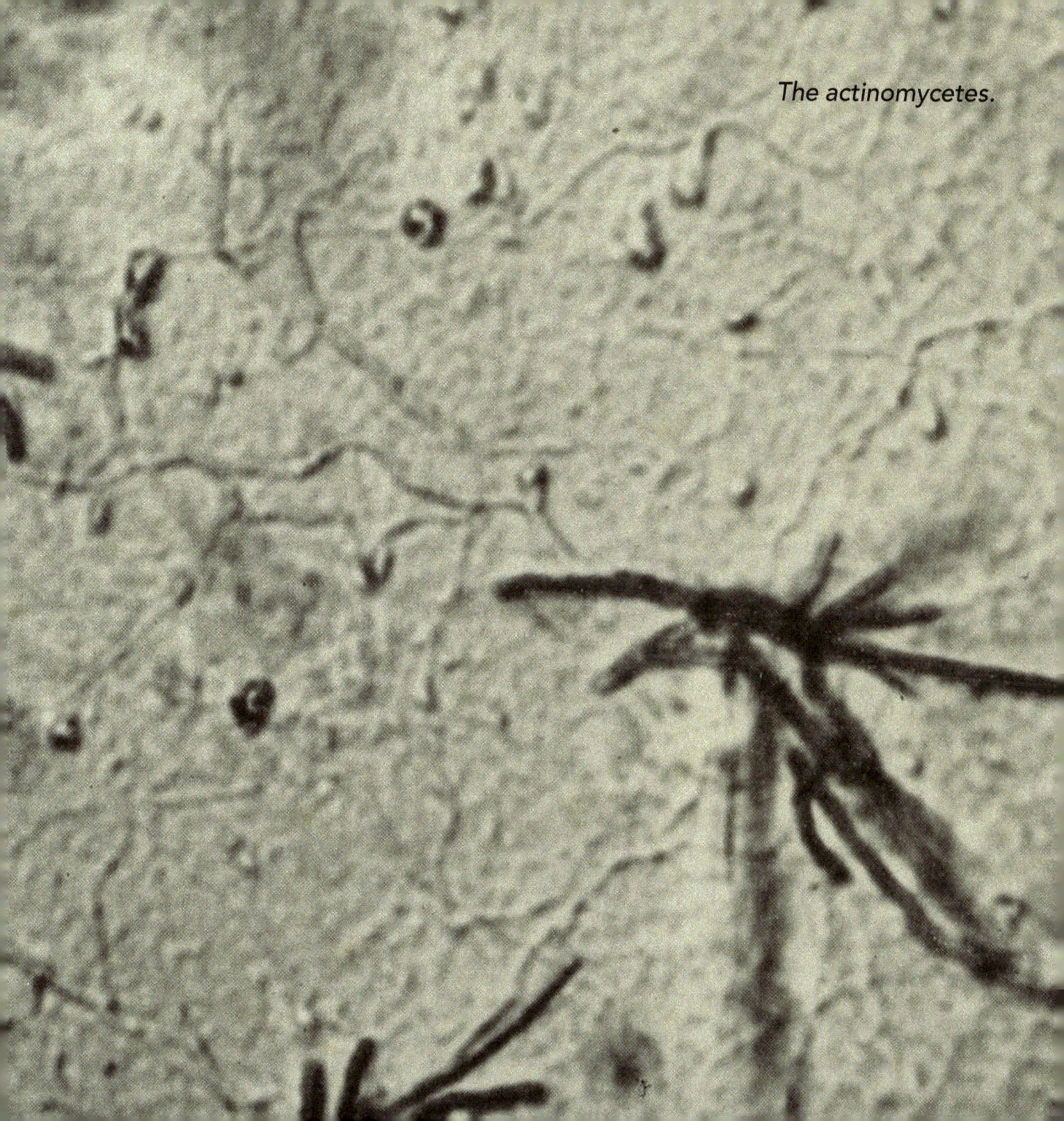

The actinomycetes.

ACTINOMYCETES

Actinomycetes are a type of bacteria but they fall in a separate category because they have similar characteristics to fungi. Their shapes as well as their branching properties are like those of fungi. They form long filaments that stretch through soil. They also decompose material in a similar way as fungi. However, like bacteria, their cells don't have a defined nucleus.

Actinomycetes have three very important functions.

- They provide us with many important antibiotics used in medicine.

- They fix nitrogen, which means they convert nitrogen from the air so plants can use it.

- They decompose tough materials, such as plant tissues, such as paper, stems from plants, and bark from trees. They can even decompose the hard exoskeletons of insects!

Scientists discovered that actinomycetes somehow kept the populations of bacterial in soil in balance. This led two scientists, named **Selman Waksman** and **Albert Shatz** to think that these microorganisms could be used to fight diseases caused by bacteria, such as tuberculosis. Their research led to lots of medicines used to fight bacterial diseases.

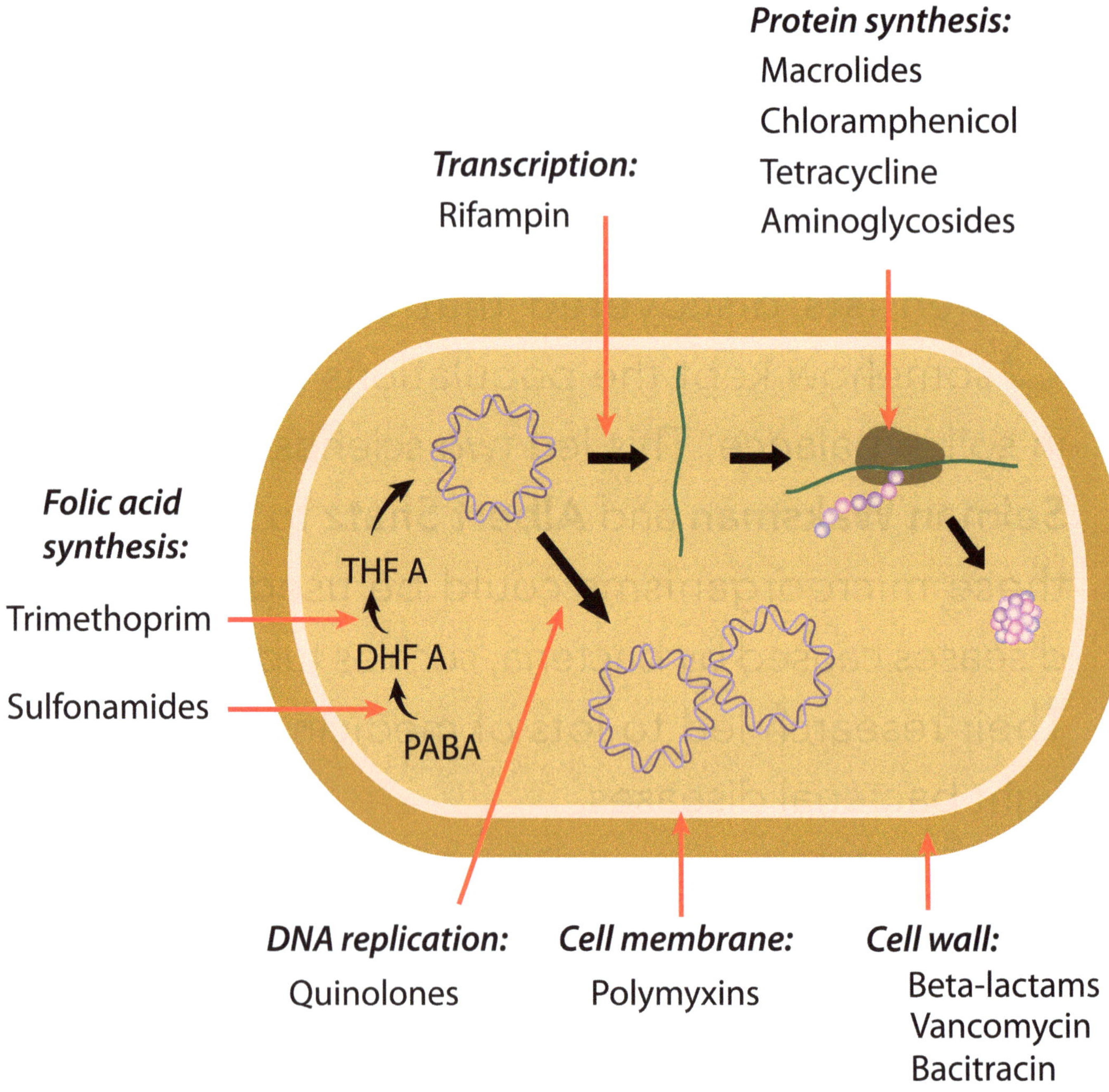
Protein synthesis:
Macrolides
Chloramphenicol
Tetracycline
Aminoglycosides
Transcription:
Rifampin
Folic acid synthesis:
THF A
Trimethoprim
DHF A
Sulfonamides
PABA
DNA replication:
Quinolones
Cell membrane:
Polymyxins
Cell wall:
Beta-lactams
Vancomycin
Bacitracin

Actinomycetes are responsible for two-thirds of the antibiotics we use today. Here are a few examples of these healing antibiotics:

- **Streptomycin,** used to treat tuberculosis

- **Neomycin,** used to reduce bacterial infection during surgery

- **Erythromycin,** used to treat bronchitis and pneumonia

- **Tetracycline,** used to heal urinary tract infections

Antibiotic sites of action.

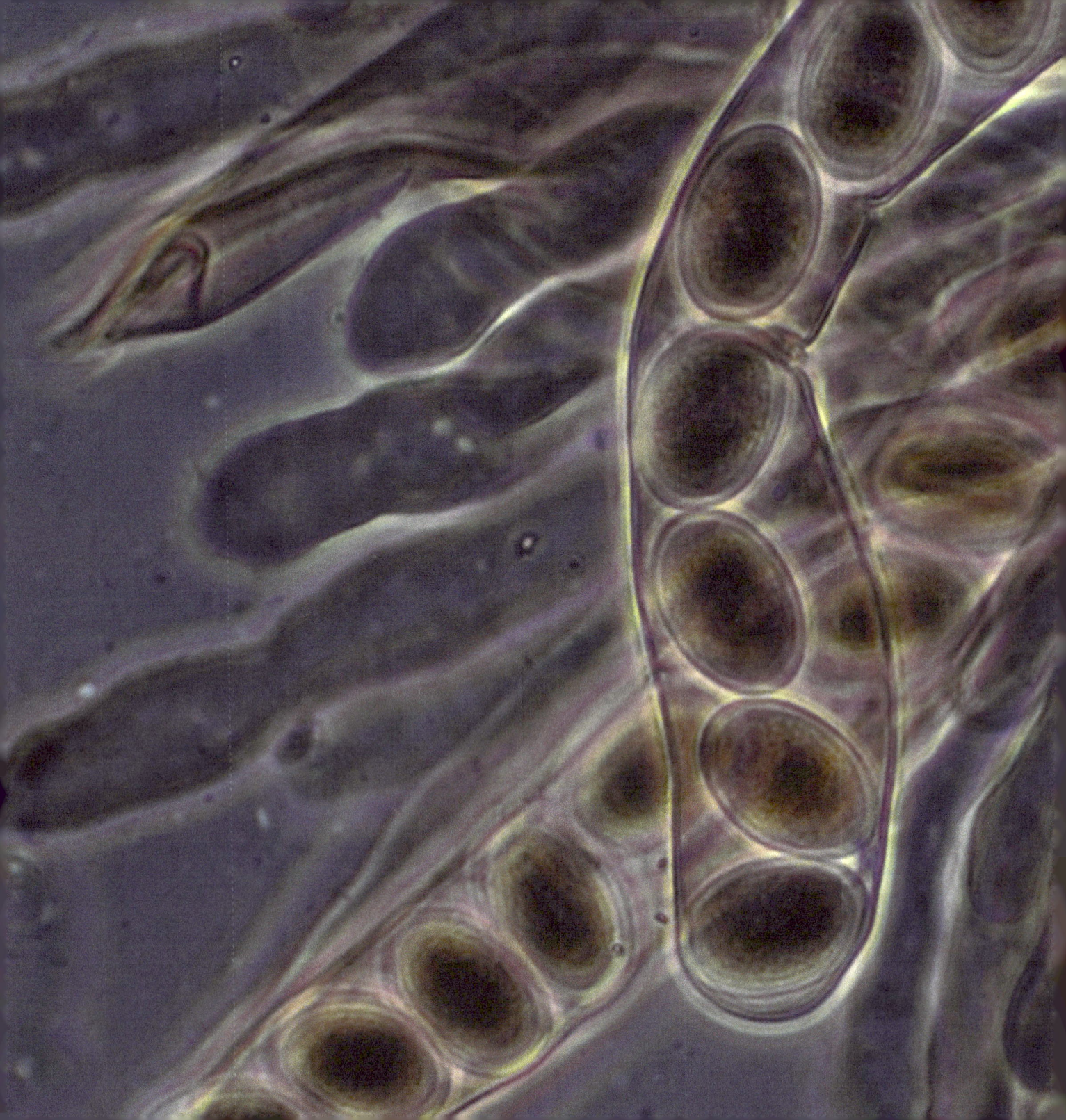

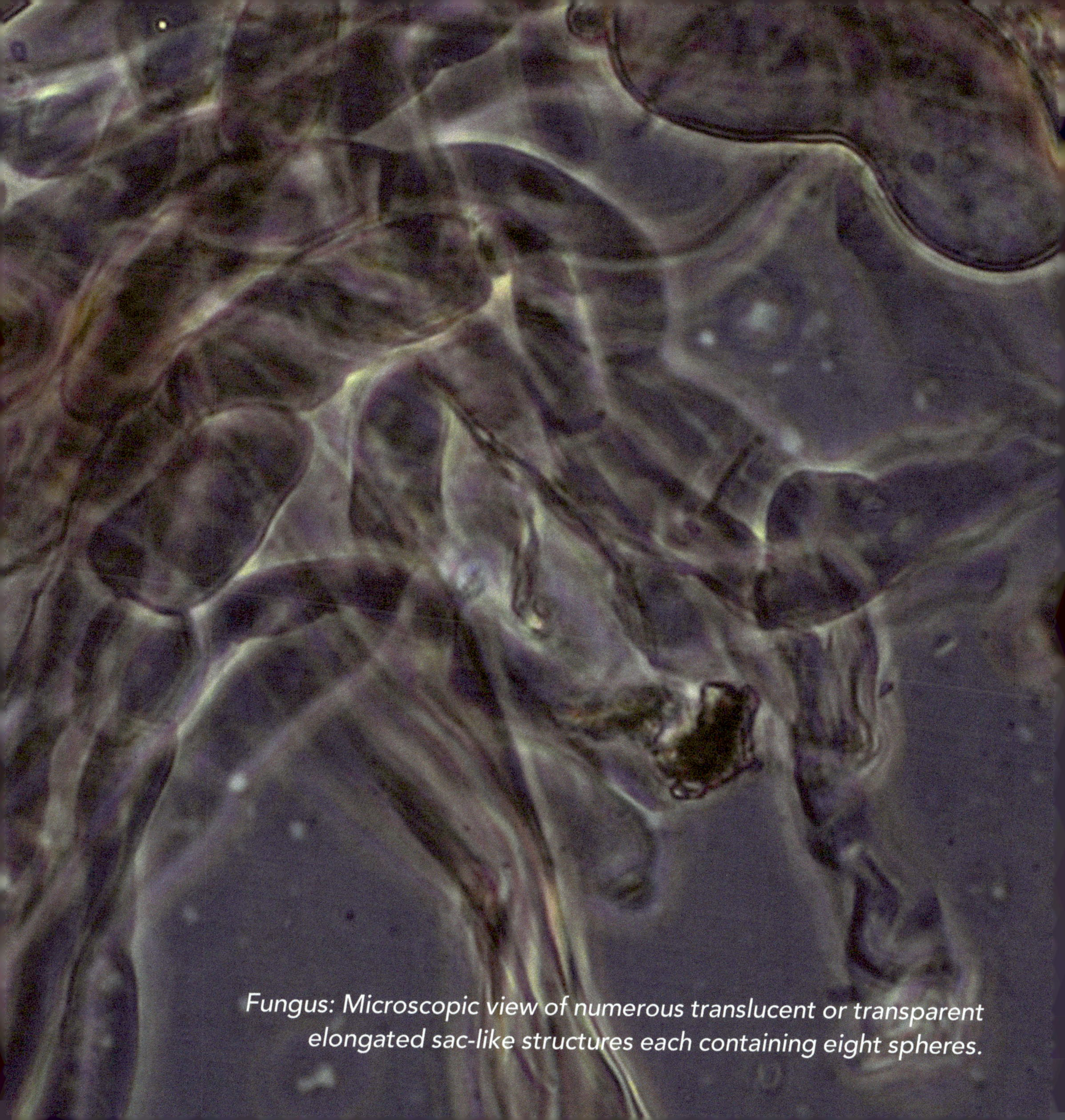

Fungus: Microscopic view of numerous translucent or transparent elongated sac-like structures each containing eight spheres.

FUNGI

Bacteria are more abundant than fungi in soil, but fungi are next in abundance. **Fungi** have eukaryote cells like animals and plants, so they're not related to bacteria, which have much simpler cells. The cells of fungi have a nucleus and other organelles. For a long time, scientists thought that fungi were a type of plants, but it was found that they differ from plants in two very important ways. Their cell walls are made of *Chitin* like the exoskeletons of certain types of animals. Also, they don't make their own food using photosynthesis like plants do.

Fungi have enzymes on the outsides of their bodies instead of stomach enzymes like we have in our stomachs. Because of this they are able to decompose animal and plant material in the soil and use it for food. There are over 75,000 different species of fungi that range in size from microscopic to measuring over 2 miles across. They can be split into species based on their shape, color, size of their spores, which they use for reproduction.

Yellow Antler Fungus - Calocera viscosa.

Bacteria and actinomycetes don't do well in environments that have a lot of acid, but fungi thrive in acidic environments. Fungi need organic matter to survive so the amount of organic matter in the soil influences the population of fungi.

Fungi are important to the soil in numerous ways:

- They are food sources for other organisms.

- They play an important part in decomposition. They break down dead organic matter with their enzymes. While they use that matter for their nutrients, they release oxygen, carbon, and nitrogen into the air. These elements are vital for the health of soil as well as the health of all living organisms.

- Like actinomycetes, some fungi are vitally important in medicines. Penicillin, an antibiotic that kills bacterial infections, is made from fungi.

Algae cell.

ALGAE

Algae are plants. They range from the single-celled forms found in soil to the large masses of seaweed found in the oceans. Like other plants, they contain chlorophyll, which means they can make their own food, but they don't have the stems, roots, leaves, or vascular tissue of most plants.

Most single-celled algae live in water but some live in soil that's moist. Soil algae fall into four main classes:

- **Cyanophyta,** which are blue-green algae

- **Chlorophyta,** which are grass-green algae

- **Xanthophyta,** which are yellow-green algae

- **Bacillariophyta,** which are golden-brown algae or diatoms

Grass-green algae and golden-brown algae can be found in temperate regions, while blue-green algae is abundant in moist, tropical soils.

Algae have many different functions in the soil.

- They play a major role in the fertility of the soil.

- When they die, they add organic matter to the soil, which enriches it

- They act as cementing agents to bind soil together.

- Through the process of photosynthesis they create oxygen to the soil and atmosphere.

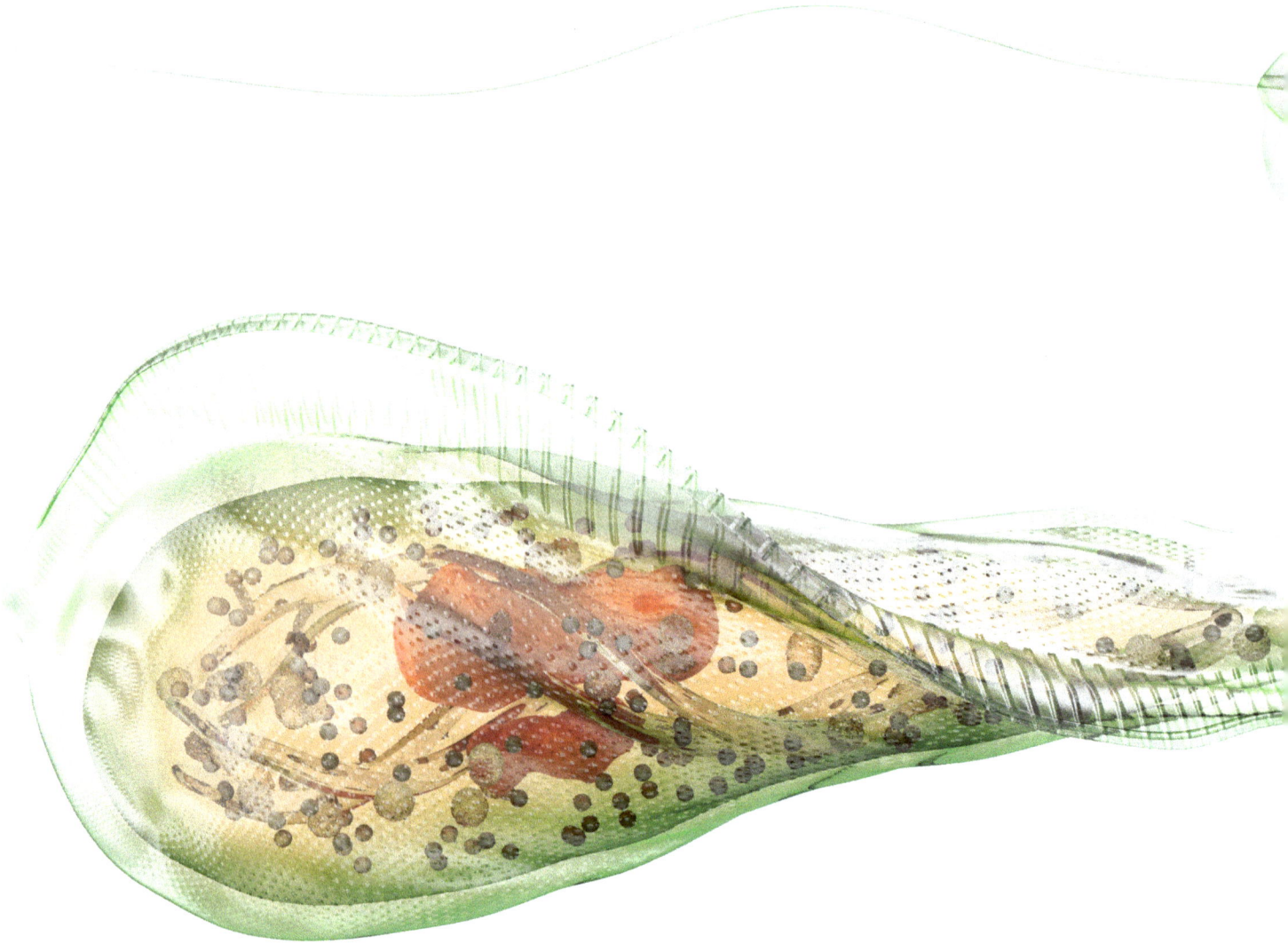

Flagellate protozoa microorganisms.

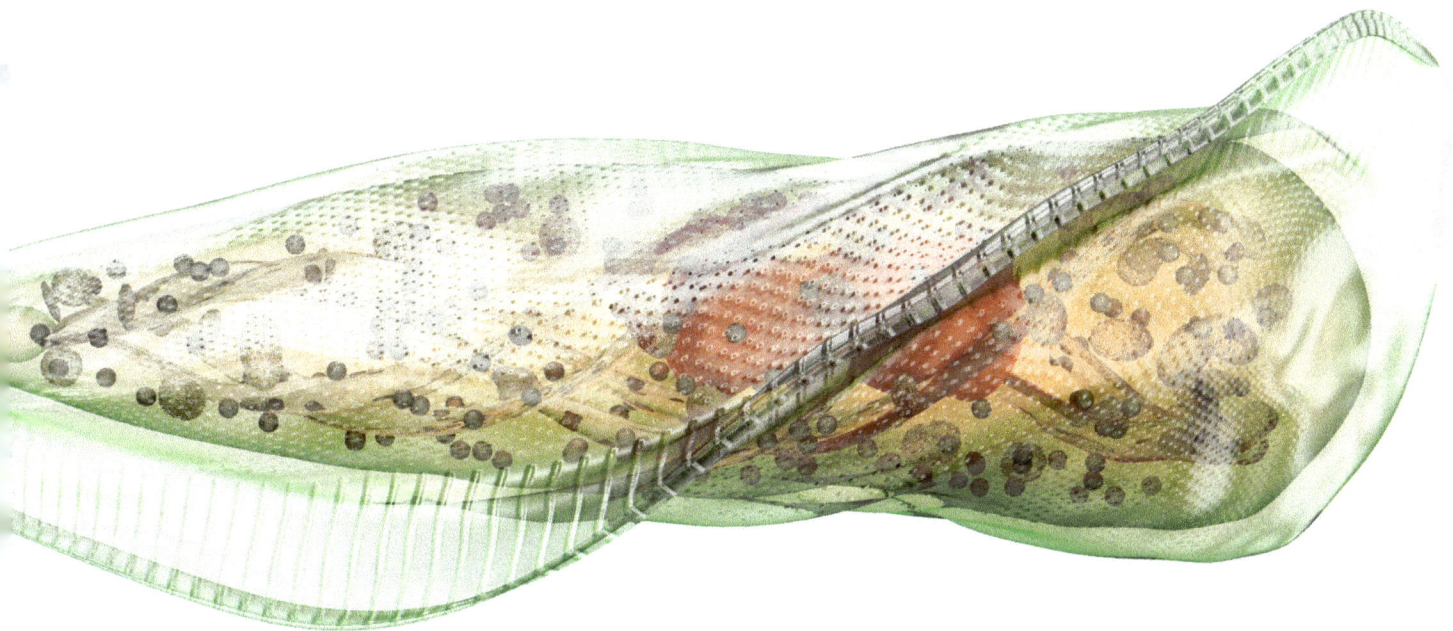

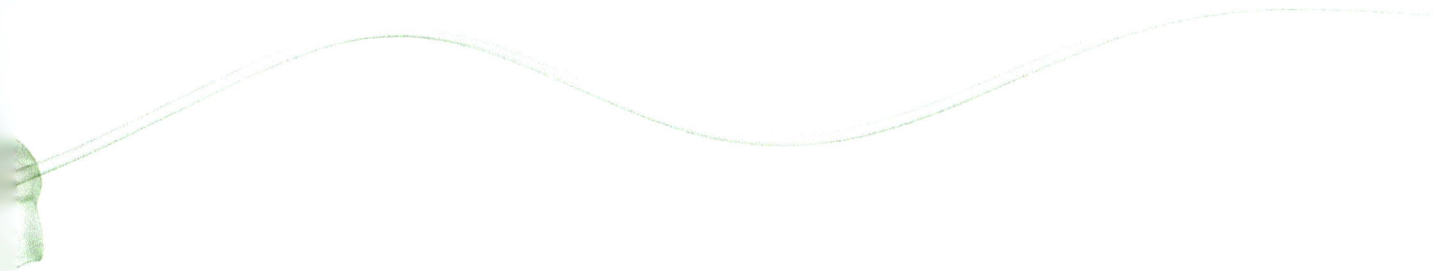

PROTOZOA

Protozoa are microorganisms that have eukaryote cells. They were some of the first microorganisms to have sexual reproduction instead of reproduction using spores.

There are three categories of protozoa:

- **Flagellates,** the smallest in size

- **Amoebae,** the middle size

- **Ciliates,** the largest size

The flagellates that are found in soil don't contain chlorophyll. The types of flagellates that do contain chlorophyll are generally found in water instead of soil. Flagellates move using flagella. Some have several and some have only one that looks like a long, whip-like appendage.

Amoebae are larger than flagellates and they move in a slug-like manner. An amoeba can alter its shape to protrude a slimy *"false foot"* that helps it move or pull in food.

Single-celled flagellate microorganisms and amoeba.

The largest of the organisms in the protozoa group, ciliates move by numerous cilia that look similar to short hairs. They give the organism more ways to move than the other types of protozoa.

Protozoa are several times larger than bacteria and they eat them, which helps to keep the population of bacteria in check. As the protozoa eat bacteria, they release excess nitrogen that is then available for plants and animals.

Paramecium caudatum is a genus of unicellular ciliated protozoa and Bacterium under the microscope.

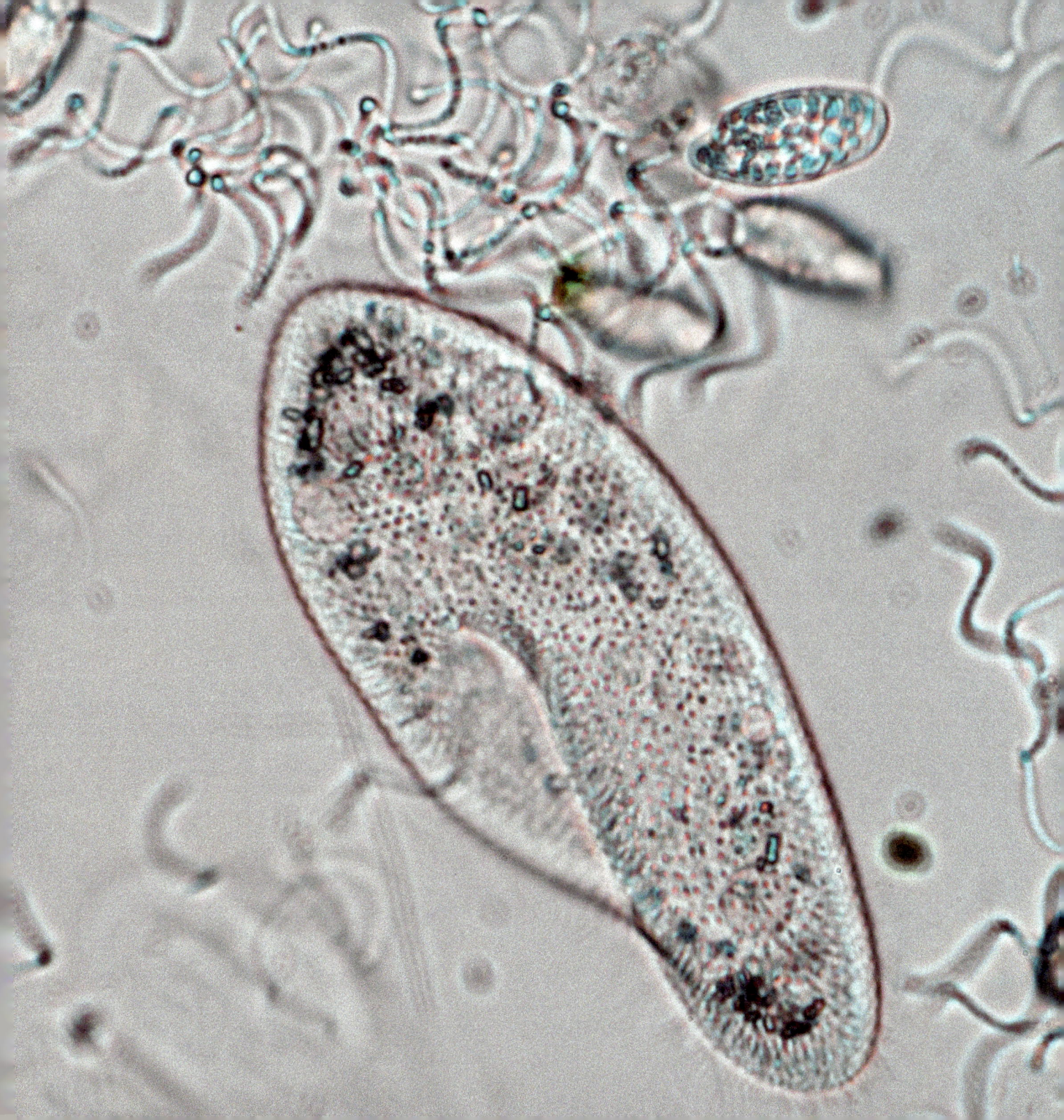

Root-knot nematodes.

NEMATODES

Nematodes are worms that are not segmented. They are about 1/20 of an inch long and 1/500 of an inch in diameter. There are a few nematodes that are responsible for plant diseases but most nematodes are beneficial.

Nematodes are very important to the food web of the soil. Some eat plants and algae. Some eat fungi and bacteria and some eat other nematodes. Like protozoa they release nutrients in forms that plants can use.

The next time you hold some soil in your hand you'll think about the millions of organisms that live in it!

Awesome! Now you more about the tiny organisms that live in soil and what they do. You can find more Books about Earth Science from Baby Professor by searching the website of your favorite book retailer.

Visit

BABY PROFESSOR
EDUCATION KIDS

www.BabyProfessorBooks.com

to download Free Baby Professor eBooks
and view our catalog of new and exciting
Children's Books

Milton Keynes UK
Ingram Content Group UK Ltd.
UKHW051146030924
447802UK00003B/354

9 798869 411716